The Concise Illustrated Book
Mushrooms and other Fungi

David Pegler

GALLERY BOOKS
An imprint of W. H. Smith Publishers Inc.
112 Madison Avenue
New York, New York 10016

First published in the United States of America
by GALLERY BOOKS
An imprint of W. H. Smith Publishers Inc.
112 Madison Avenue
New York, New York 10016

ISBN 0-8317-6193-8

Printed in the German Democratic Republic

Acknowledgments
All photographs from Images Colour Library
except for the following: Gordon Dickson 10, 11,
13, 18, 19, 24, 27, 29, 33, 38, 42, 46; Roger
Phillips 35.

All artworks supplied by Maltings Partnership

Right: Crested Clavaria (see page 44).

CONTENTS

Introduction

Mushrooms and toadstools are names given to a large group of gill-bearing, fleshy fungi, which are collectively given the scientific name of 'agarics' (order *Agaricales*). There are about four thousand agarics in the Northern Hemisphere, and many more thousands in the tropical and subtropical forests. The Fungi form a Kingdom in their own right, comparable to Plants and Animals, and, apart from the agarics, they include a great variety of forms. These include puff-balls, jelly fungi, cup-fungi, bracket-fungi, club-fungi, rusts and smuts, yeasts, moulds and many other fungi that cause disease in animals and plants. The study of fungi is called *mycology*.

Fungi greatly affect our everyday lives. Yeasts are used in baking and brewing, antibiotics are produced from certain fungi, pathogens affect the farmer's crops, the Dry Rot Fungus and others damage your house, and there are many uses of fungi in biotechnology.

Like all fungi, mushrooms consist of fine, microscopic threads, called *hyphae*, which grow and branch within the soil or other substratum to form a *mycelium*. When climatic conditions are appropriate, there comes a need to produce spores which can be disseminated, usually by the wind, in order to spread the species. The mushroom or toadstool is a type of fruitbody, in which the spores are produced.

The structure of a mushroom is therefore designed to enable the production and release of the microscopic spores, and the spore-bearing parts must be protected while this process is carried out. A mushroom then is essentially either an umbrella, to keep off the rain, or a parasol, to keep out the heat of the sun. There are three main parts to a mushroom: the *cap* which forms an upper protective layer, the *stem* (or *stipe*) which lifts the spore-producing region above ground level so that the released spores are carried away by air currents, and the *gills*, which radiate out on the underside of the cap and produce the spores. In addition, in some mushrooms there are additional protective layers, called *veils*, which gradually break down as the mushroom expands.

Mushrooms grow very quickly, and their sudden appearance has resulted in a great deal of mystic folklore. Growth is not magical however, but is due to a very rapid uptake of water which quickly expands the hyphae of the mushroom flesh. A typical mushroom is about 90 per cent water, so they tend to rot very easily and disappear almost as fast as they appear.

The appearance and structure of the

parts of a mushroom are important in its scientific classification, and you will use these features in the field to identify your finds. The *cap* has precise characteristics regarding its size, shape (which can change with age), colour, texture and the presence of remnants of the veil. The *stem* will have similar features, and it is always important to pick the base. Also check in what type of surroundings and on what it is growing. The *gills* also have to be studied with care, especially in the way they are attached to the top of the stem, for which special terms are used. When the gills do not reach the stem but leave an intervening space they are described as *free*. They are described as *adnexed* when they just reach the stem, as *adnate* when they are attached by their full width, and *decurrent* when they run down the stem a good way. Finally, some gills curve upwards just before reaching the stem and these are called *sinuate*. The veils may form a thin *ring* of tissue or a cobweb-like *cortina* on the upper part of the stem, or a sack-like *volva* at the base, out of which the stem grows. Species of *Amanita* often have both structures.

Modern scientific thinking on the relationships, origins and classification of mushrooms very much depends upon recognition of detailed structure observed under a powerful microscope. Most important are the spores and for this reason details of these are given in the following pages. The spores often have a characteristic colour when brought together in large numbers, and this can easily be seen by making a *spore-print*. Spore-prints are produced by removing the cap from the stem and placing it gill side downwards on a piece of paper. After a few hours, sufficient spores will be released to leave a coloured print, outlining the arrangement of the gills. Spore-prints should always be taken when you are unsure of the identification.

The terms 'mushroom' and 'toadstool' have been used for many years and the difference between them has long been lost. The traditional distinction that mushrooms are edible and toadstools are poisonous no longer holds true, as more is discovered about them. The Commercial Mushroom, which is so familiar in greengrocers and markets, belongs to the genus *Agaricus*, so the term mushroom is sometimes confined to *Agaricus* species, but not all *Agaricus* species are edible (see the Yellow-staining Mushroom, p. 33). Many wild 'toadstools' are edible, however, and are much prized, more so in eastern and central Europe than in Britain and North America. On the other hand, of course, there are poisonous wild mushrooms and toadstools, and some are **deadly poisonous**. If you plan to explore the many species which grow naturally in our woods and fields, and especially if you are planning to collect wild mushrooms for the table, then **remember** the following:

1 Never take a risk; if you are at all in doubt of your identification then leave it alone.
2 A beginner must always get his finds identified by an expert. There are many local natural history societies which arrange 'fungus forays' with experts present. Every country has its national Mycological Society which can often offer help.
3 Keep the different species separate, so they do not become mixed.
4 Wash your hands before eating anything.
5 Finally, learn to recognize the Death Cap (p. 12) first.

BLUSHER

Amanita rubescens

Description: Variable in appearance. *Cap* 5–15cm (2–6in) diameter, convex to depressed but sometimes with raised centre, greyish to reddish brown, often with olive tints, smooth but sticky when wet, bearing small, greyish patches of veil which can be washed away by rain. *Gills* free, whitish but bruising reddish brown, broad and crowded. *Stem* 7–20cm ($2\frac{3}{4}$–8in), 1–2cm ($\frac{1}{3}$–$\frac{2}{3}$in) thick, with a swollen base but lacking a volva, smooth, fibrous, white bruising dirty pinkish. *Ring* present on upper stem but collapsing, white, thin. *Flesh* whitish but soon turning pink on exposure. *Spore-print* white; *spores* colourless, smooth, staining blue in iodine.

Edibility: Best avoided. Poisonous if eaten raw, causing breakdown of red blood cells, but can be eaten if well cooked.

General remarks: One of the most common woodland species. The English name refers to the pink discoloration of the flesh when exposed, which is especially apparent around insect holes. Do not confuse this species with the very poisonous Panther (*A. pantherina*) which does not bruise, has white, not grey, veil patches on the cap, and ring-like remains of a veil on stem base. The rarer Tall Amanita (*A. excelsa*) is similar but has a much longer stem.

Classification: Basidiomycotina, family Amanitaceae.
Habitat: On ground, in mixed woods, especially oak and conifers.
Distribution: Widespread, throughout Northern Hemisphere.
Season: Late June–October (February–April on West Coast of U.S.A.).

Paxillus involutus

Classification: Basidiomycotina, family Paxillaceae.

Habitat: On poor soils and damp litter, especially in birch woods, often in groups.

Distribution: Widespread in Northern Hemisphere, especially northern and mountainous regions.

Season: June–December.

Description: *Cap* 5–15cm (2–6in) diameter, rarely larger, convex then depressed in centre, yellowish brown to rusty brown, felt-like texture but slimy when wet. *Gills* decurrent, cream to reddish yellow, with rusty spots, soft and moist, easily pulled away from cap. *Stem* 3–7cm ($1\frac{1}{4}$–$2\frac{3}{4}$in) long, solid, pale then bruising dark brown. *Flesh* soft, pale cream. *Spore-print* clay-brown; *spores* ellipsoid, smooth.

Edibility: Avoid. Although this mushroom is frequently eaten in eastern Europe, it may cause cumulative poisoning from repeated consumption, leading to vascular collapse and kidney failure. In North America it is sometimes called the Poison Paxillus.

General remarks: Very common. The margin of the cap is strongly inrolled in young specimens and only slowly unrolls as the cap expands. *P. atrotomentosus* is more robust, and has a brown-black velvety stem. *P. panuoides* is a smaller species, forming overlapping brackets on coniferous wood, and lacking a stem. Although these species have gills, they are more closely related to the boletes.

CLOUDED AGARIC

Clitocybe nebularis

Description: *Cap* 7–16cm (2¾–6¼in) diameter, fleshy, convex to flat or with a raised centre, ash grey or with a yellowish brown tint, dry with a hoary appearance. *Gills* shortly decurrent, off-white, crowded. *Stem* 5–20cm (2–8in), up to 2.5cm (1in) thick, cylindric, same colour as cap, striate. *Flesh* thick, firm, white, with a strong, unpleasant smell of Swedish turnip. *Spore-print* creamy white; *spores* small, colourless, ellipsoid.

Edibility: Although said to be edible, it causes considerable discomfort to some individuals and should be treated with extreme caution.

General remarks: A large common mushroom, often growing in groups and forming 'fairy-rings' in the woodland humus. There are many species of *Clitocybe*, commonly found in all kinds of woodland. All have pale, decurrent gills, and are mostly dull coloured.

Classification: Basidiomycotina, family Tricholomataceae.
Habitat: Among rich humus in deciduous and coniferous woodland.
Distribution: Throughout northern Europe, Rocky Mountains and west coast of North America.
Season: August–November.

Classification: Basidiomycotina, family Russulaceae.
Habitat: In small troops, usually amongst grass in beech woods.
Distribution: Fairly common throughout Europe and North America.
Season: June–October.

Russula virescens

Description: *Cap* 5–12cm (2–4¾in) diameter, convex then expanding, finally depressed in centre, colour varying from greyish green to olive-brown, dry, and finally cracking into small scales especially at the edge. *Gills* adnate, creamy white, rather brittle and fairly crowded. *Stem* 4–8cm (1½–3in) long, up to 3cm (1¼in) thick, solid, white. *Flesh* thick, crumbly, white, with a fruity smell and a mild taste. *Spore-print* cream; *spores* ovoid, colourless, ornamented with warts and a partial network which stains blue in iodine.
Edibility: A mild-tasting *Russula* species which is regarded as excellent to eat with a nutty flavour. Remember to avoid confusion with the Death Cap (p. 12).
General remarks: This is one of the few *Russula* species sold as food in central European markets. The cracked surface is useful in identification, as is the taste. Green colour is unusual in mushrooms and toadstools, for unlike plants they do not contain chlorophyll. However, there are several green *Russula* species: the common *R. cyanoxantha*, normally greyish purple, has a green form and white gills; *R. heterophylla* is rarer, with forking, crowded gills; the Grass-green Russula (*R. aeruginea*) grows under birch trees, and has a yellowish green cap which does not crack.

DEATH CAP

Amanita phalloides

Description: *Cap* 6–15cm (2½–6in) diameter, convex then slowly expanding, olive-green in centre becoming yellowish green towards the edge, satiny, radially streaked, occasionally with attached whitish patches of veil. *Gills* free white and remaining so, crowded. *Stem* 7–20cm (2¾–8in), up to 1.5cm (¾in) thick, white, cylindric and arising from a thin, white, cup-like volva at base, also bearing a white, persistent ring on the upper part. *Flesh* thick, white, with a honey-like smell which soon becomes unpleasant (like ammonia). *Spore-print* white; *spores* colourless, ovoid, blue in iodine.

Edibility: Deadly poisonous, the most dangerous species of all, even when cooked. Invariably fatal. Hands should be washed immediately after contact.

General remarks: The beginner **must** learn to recognize this mushroom. Pale specimens can be confused with the Horse Mushroom (p. 21), so always check for the white gills and the ring and volva. The False Death Cap (*A. citrina*) is commoner, with a lemon-yellow to almost white cap, and a swollen base to stem. Replaced in the north by the Destroying Angel (*A. virosa*) which is just as deadly, but is pure white with a slender scaly stem.

Classification: Basidiomycotina, family Amanitaceae.
Habitat: On ground in oak and beech woods.
Distribution: Widespread but only locally common, rare or absent in more northern regions.
Season: July–November.

Marasmius oreades

Classification: Basidiomycotina, family Tricholomataceae.
Habitat: In grassland, on lawns, grass verges and meadows.
Distribution: Widespread throughout Northern Hemisphere.
Season: May–November.

Description: *Cap* 2–5cm (¾–2in) diameter, bell-shaped or convex with a raised central area, pale pinkish to yellow brown, smooth, with a grooved edge. *Gills* adnexed, whitish, broad, widely spaced. *Stem* 4–6cm (1½–2½in), about 2–3mm (⅛in) thick, slender, pale yellowish brown, fibrous. *Flesh* thin, white. *Spore-print* white; *spores* colourless, ovoid, smooth.

Edibility: Although the fruitbodies are small and not very fleshy, this is generally regarded as good to eat. Normally added to stews and casseroles, but also excellent when fried after discarding the fibrous stems. Take care to avoid *Clitocybe dealbata* which grows in similar situations but is poisonous, containing the alkaloid muscarine. It is whitish grey, with crowded, decurrent gills.

General remarks: A familiar small mushroom, well known to gardeners as fruitbodies frequently form large and persistent 'fairy-rings' on otherwise well tended lawns. Many fairy-rings are hundreds of years old and increase in size every year. They are difficult to eradicate, owing to the extensive underground mycelium which grows continuously. *Marasmius* species are generally small and tough. They revive when moistened, so tend to persist longer.

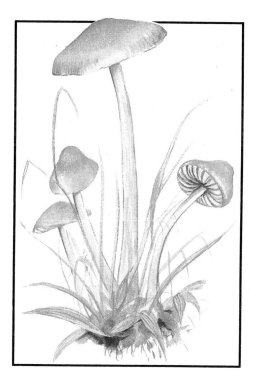

FAWN PLUTEUS

Pluteus cervinus (P. atricapillus)

Description: *Cap* 3–12cm (1¼–4¾in) diameter, strongly convex, greyish brown to dark brown, radially streaky, dry but can become sticky when moist. *Gills* free, at first whitish then becoming a deep flesh-pink colour, broad, densely crowded. *Stem* 6–10cm (2½–4in), about 1cm (⅜in) thick, cylindric, white, with fine, longitudinal, dark brown fibrils, especially on the lower half. *Flesh* whitish, soft and watery, soon decaying. *Spore-print* salmon pink; *spores* round, smooth, with thickened wall.

Edibility: Can be eaten but considered of poor quality.

General remarks: The most common of about 30 species of *Pluteus*, often found in groups of two or three. *Pluteus* species are recognized by the pink, free gills. Other common species include the Willow Pluteus (*P. salicinus*) with a greenish to bluish grey cap, and *P. lutescens* with a brownish cap and chrome yellow stem.

Classification: Basidiomycotina, family Pluteaceae.

Habitat: On stumps, fallen trunks and sawdust heaps, in deciduous woods.

Distribution: Very common everywhere.

Season: January–December, but more frequent in Autumn.

Agaricus campestris

Classification: Basidiomycotina, family Agaricaceae.
Habitat: In grassland, meadows, but never in woods.
Distribution: Widespread, throughout Northern Hemisphere.
Season: July–October.

Description: *Cap* 3–8cm ($1\frac{1}{4}$–$3\frac{1}{4}$in) diameter, convex then expanding to become flat, with a pure white surface which breaks up to form indefinite concentric scales, and a ragged, incurved edge. *Gills* free, initially white soon pink then finally deep chocolate brown, broad, crowded. *Stem* 4–6cm ($1\frac{1}{2}$–$2\frac{1}{2}$in), up to 1.5cm ($\frac{5}{8}$in) thick, short, cylindric but tapering at base, white, bearing thin, often very poorly developed ring on the upper half. *Flesh* thick, firm, white, tending to discolour reddish, especially in the stem, when exposed. *Spore-print* purplish brown; *spores* small, ovoid, dark brown, smooth.
Edibility: Excellent, but always check that the gills darken, and that there is a ring but no volva on the stem.
General remarks: Although the short, squat Field Mushroom is always used as a textbook example, it is less common than some other *Agaricus* species. It is often thought to have a more nutty flavour than the Commercial Mushroom (*A. bisporus*), which is closely related and often confused. True mushrooms either have flesh which reddens when broken, as in the Field Mushroom, or the surface bruises yellow, as in the case of the Yellow-staining Mushroom (p. 33).

FLY AGARIC

Amanita muscaria

Description: *Cap* 10–25cm (4–10in) diameter, convex, flat or depressed in centre, bright scarlet red fading to orange, at first covered by a thick, white, fluffy veil which breaks up to produce indefinite rings of wart-like scales. Scales can become washed away by rain. *Gills* free or almost free, white, broad, crowded. *Stem* 10–20cm (4–8in), up to 2cm (¾in) thick, cylindric but swelling at base, bearing a white to cream hanging ring, and white scales at base which represent the volva. *Flesh* thick, firm, white, unchanging. *Spore-print* white; *spores* ellipsoid, colourless, not staining blue in iodine.

Edibility: Poisonous, and should be avoided. It contains two toxins, minute amounts of *muscimol* which can produce psychotropic illness, and *muscarine* which causes excessive sweating and poses a more serious risk.

General remarks: The name Fly Agaric originates from its use, particularly in eastern Europe as a fly-killer. Cut up and placed in milk, flies feeding on this are stupefied. Its supposed hallucinatory properties have led to the belief that the Vikings used it as an intoxicant, and it might represent 'Soma', the divine plant of immortality of ancient Asian cultures.

Classification: Basidiomycotina, family Amanitaceae.
Habitat: On ground, under birch, pine, and spruce.
Distribution: Common throughout Northern Hemisphere, although rarer on the east coast of North America.
Season: August–November.

Russula foetens

Classification: Basidiomycotina, family Russulaceae.
Habitat: On the ground, in deciduous or mixed woodland.
Distribution: Northern Europe and the more southern states of the U.S.A., where it is less common.
Season: June–October.

Description: *Cap* 10–18cm (4–7in) diameter, strongly rounded when young and never expanding to more than convex, dull yellowish brown, smooth and very slimy, especially in wet weather, with a strongly grooved edge. *Gills* adnate, off-white developing brown spots, broad, crowded. *Stem* 10–13cm (4–5in), 2–4cm ($\frac{3}{4}$–1$\frac{1}{2}$in) thick, whitish, hollow and very brittle. *Flesh* white, crumbly, bruising red, with a hot, peppery taste and a strong rancid smell. *Spore-print*: cream; *spores* ovoid, colourless, covered with warts which stain blue in iodine.
Edibility: Not inedible but the hot peppery taste is unpleasant and likely to result in stomach upsets.
General remarks: A large, robust species, easily recognized by the slimy cap and the unpleasant smell. *R. laurocerasi* is similar but smells of marzipan, whilst *R. sororia* also has a grooved cap-edge but is smaller and greyer. Species of *Russula* (Brittle-gills) and *Lactarius* (Milk Caps) form a large family of woodland mushrooms with fleshy fruitbodies. They are often brightly coloured and have very brittle flesh which crumbles when squashed. Each species grows with a particular tree, and identification also usually involves knowing whether they taste mild or peppery.

GRISETTE

Amanita vaginata

Description: *Cap* 3–8cm (1¼–3¼in) diameter, conical to bell-shaped and only finally expanding to become flat with a raised centre, grey and often darker at centre, with a strongly striated edge, and devoid of any scales from the veil. *Gills* free, white, broad, crowded. *Stem* 10–20cm (4–8in), up to 1cm (½in) thick, elongate, cylindrical, hollow, white with greyish zones, arising from a large white, membranous, cup-like volva, but lacking a ring. *Flesh* thin, white, unchanging. *Spore-print* white; *spores* spherical, colourless, not staining blue with iodine.

Edibility: Said to be good to eat *after* cooking, but contains haemolysins which can attack the blood and cause anaemia if it is eaten fresh.

General remarks: The Grisettes are a distinctive group of *Amanita* species, recognized by their tall, elegant form, and by the absence of a ring on the stem. There are several species, mostly differing in colour, the most common being the Tawny Grisette (*A. fulva*) which has a bright tawny brown cap.

Classification: Basidiomycotina, family Amanitaceae.

Habitat: On the ground in both coniferous and deciduous woodland, especially birch.

Distribution: Very common throughout the Northern Hemisphere, even extending into the Arctic Circle.

Season: June–October (November–February in western U.S.A.).

Rozites caperata

Classification: Basidiomycotina, family Cortinariaceae.

Habitat: On acid, sandy soils in beech and coniferous woods.

Distribution: Locally common in Europe and North America, preferring more northerly and mountainous localities.

Season: August–October.

Description: *Cap* 6–12cm (2½–4¾in) diameter, convex, soon becoming flattened with an undulating wrinkled edge, straw yellow or duller, dry, with a hoary aspect. *Gills* adnate, with a tooth, light brown, broad, vertically wrinkled, crowded. *Stem* 10–15cm (4–6in), about 2cm (¾in) thick, cylindric, white to yellowish, with longitudinal fibres, and bearing a thin white ring on the upper part which eventually becomes broken. *Flesh* thick, white, with a pleasant smell. *Spore-print* rusty brown; *spores* almond-shaped, brown, with a warty ornament.

Edibility: Although this mushroom is bitter when raw, this taste disappears on cooking and it is much admired as an edible species, especially in central Europe. Do not mistake for the many *Cortinarius* species.

General remarks: This is rare in some countries and in Britain is only found occasionally in Scotland, but it is very common throughout Scandinavia. It either grows singly or in large troops. *R. caperata* is the only species found in the Northern Hemisphere, and is closely related to the genus *Cortinarius*, of which there are more than 400 species. *Cortinarius* species are recognized by the cobwebby veil (cortina) which covers the very young gills.

HONEY FUNGUS

Armillaria mellea

Description: *Cap* 5–12cm (2–4¾in) diameter, convex then flattened, yellowish to tawny brown, paler towards edge, bearing small, dark, hair-like scales concentrated towards the centre but sparse towards edge. *Gills* shortly decurrent, off-white or staining pinkish, crowded. *Stem* 10–15cm (4–6in), up to 2cm (¾in) thick, cylindric, tough, pale brown but paler towards top, bearing a thick, cottony, white ring with yellow scales. *Flesh* white, soft, with a sharp, bitter taste. *Spore-print* cream; *spores* colourless, ovoid, smooth.

Edibility: Young specimens are regarded as edible when well cooked, and after rejecting the tough stems. Some people, however, find the taste too bitter, whilst others show an allergic reaction.

General remarks: Also called the Bootlace Fungus because it spreads by dark black cords (rhizomorphs) under the tree bark. It is a serious parasite and kills many broad-leaved trees. Several species of Honey Fungus are recognized. *A. ostoyae* has a pinkish cap and gills, a ring with brown scales, and attacks mainly conifers. *A. bulbosa* is smaller, with a bulbous stem base and poorly developed ring, and only attacks already weak trees.

Classification: Basidiomycotina, family Tricholomataceae.
Habitat: In clusters on wood. At base of living and dead trees, stumps, and from buried wood.
Distribution: Widespread and common, throughout Europe and North America.
Season: June–November.

Agaricus arvensis

Classification: Basidiomycotina, family Agaricaceae.
Habitat: In open grassland, meadows, fields, sometimes forming 'fairy-rings'.
Distribution: Throughout the Northern Hemisphere.
Season: June–December, (November–April in western U.S.A.).

Description: *Cap* 6–20cm (2½–8in) diameter, strongly convex gradually expanding to become flattened, white to cream, discolours pale yellow on handling. *Gills* free, at first white, soon brownish and finally dark chocolate brown, crowded. *Stem* easily separated from cap, 8–12cm (3¼–4¾in), up to 2cm (¾in) thick, cylindric, sometimes with slightly swollen base, white, bearing a large, thick, hanging ring towards top. *Flesh* thick, white, unchanging, with an aniseed smell. *Spore-print* purplish brown; *spores* ovoid, dark brown, smooth.
Edibility: A wild mushroom of outstanding flavour.
General remarks: Although the surface will discolour yellow, do not mistake it for the Yellow-staining Mushroom (p. 33) which must be avoided. There are about 50 species of *Agaricus* growing wild, in addition to the Commercial Mushroom. Some are confined to woodland, and others to open grassland. The Prince, *A. augustus* is one of the largest species. It also bruises yellow but has dark brown scales on cap.

21

LILAC MYCENA

Mycena pura

Description: *Cap* 2–5cm (¾–2in) diameter, bell-shaped then expanding to flat with a raised centre, pale rose pink to lilac, although colour can be washed out by rain to look almost white. Smooth, moist, with a semi-transparent edge which appears striate. *Gills* adnate, with a decurrent tooth, pinkish or paling to whitish, broad, well spaced. *Stem* 4–10cm (1½–4in), about 2–3mm (⅛in) thick, same colour as cap, sometimes twisted, smooth except for down-covered base. *Flesh* thin, translucent, with a smell and taste recalling radish. *Spore-print* white; *spores* colourless, ellipsoid, smooth, staining blue in iodine.

Edibility: Not worth bothering with, and should in any case be avoided as it is suspected of containing small amounts of the toxic alkaloid muscarine.

General remarks: There are about 150 species of *Mycena*, of which the Lilac Mycena is one of the more robust. Most are small delicate toadstools, usually growing in tufts, often on old stumps. *M. pelianthina* is similar but has a dark violet edge to gills. Some species exude a coloured juice when the stem is broken, such as the Milk-drop Mycena (*M. galopus*) with white juice, the Bleeding Mycena (*M. haematopus*) with blood-red juice, and The Stainer (*M. crocata*) with yellow juice.

Classification: Basidiomycotina, family Tricholomataceae.
Habitat: On the ground, in oak and beech woods.
Distribution: Widespread throughout the Northern Hemisphere.
Season: June–December.

OYSTER MUSHROOM

Pleurotus ostreatus

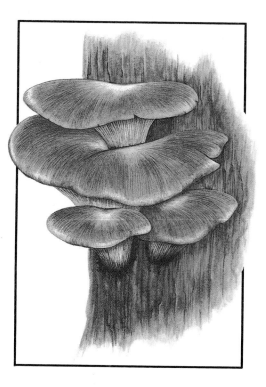

Classification: Basidiomycotina, family Polyporaceae.

Habitat: On dead wood, forming clusters on deciduous trees, especially beech, on both standing and fallen tree-trunks.

Distribution: Common throughout the Northern Hemisphere.

Season: January–December.

Description: *Cap* 5–14cm (2–5½in) diameter, bracket-shaped, convex, variable in colour from black, purplish, bluish grey through to pale buff, smooth and shiny. *Gills* decurrently attached to the sterile base, white, more or less widely spaced. *Stem* short, thick, lateral or at times absent, 2–3cm (¾–1¼in) long, whitish, solid. *Flesh* thick, firm, white. *Spore-print* pale lilac; *spores* colourless, cylindric, smooth.

Edibility: Excellent and thought by many to be the best wild mushroom, especially when young. Take care to clean it thoroughly. The species has been grown commercially for many years in eastern Europe.

General remarks: These large soft fleshed brackets have been called the 'shellfish of the woods' and may be found all the year, although the variation in colour can be confusing, with darker forms tending to appear in winter. There are several closely related species, one of the more common being the Branched Oyster Fungus (*P. cornucopiae*), which is pale, usually grows on beech and can be recognized by the gills which branch at the top of the stem. The Veiled Oyster (*P. dryinus*) has a felty surface and a membranous veil which covers the gills when young.

23

PARASOL

Macrolepiota procera

Description: *Cap* 10–30cm (8–12in) diameter, convex with a central raised hump, and with a shaggy margin. The surface breaks up from centre into rings of large, plate-like brown scales and a greyish background. *Gills* free, creamy white, broad, very crowded. *Stem* easily pulled away from cap, 15–35cm (6–14in), up to 2cm ($\frac{3}{4}$in) thick or more at the swollen base, cylindric, fibrous and hollow, covered with scaly bands resembling snake-skin, and bearing a large, thick, movable ring. *Flesh* thick, white, fleshy. *Spore-print* white; *spores* large, colourless, ellipsoid with a germ-pore, staining red-brown in iodine.

Edibility: Excellent with a nutty flavour. The stems are normally discarded. It is best cooked quickly, either grilled or fried.

General remarks: One of the largest mushrooms and easy to recognize by the pattern on the stem and large ring. The related Shaggy Parasol (*M. rhacodes*) is more stocky, the flesh discolours deep red when broken, and it usually grows on disturbed soil or compost heaps. In North America, the Green-spored Lepiota (*Chlorophyllum molybdites*) occurs and can be confused with the Parasols, but is not found in Europe.

Classification: Basidiomycotina, family Agaricaceae.

Habitat: In grass, usually in glades and at the edge of woods, sometimes in large numbers and forming 'fairy-rings'.

Distribution: Common throughout Europe, and on the eastern side of North America.

Season: July–October.

Classification: Basidiomycotina, family Tricholomataceae.
Habitat: Solitary or in clusters on conifer stumps; especially pines.
Distribution: Fairly common throughout Europe and North America.
Season: August–November, (up to February in west North America).

Description: *Cap* 5–12cm (2–5in) diameter, strongly convex or with a raised centre, almost flat when fully expanded, yellow but densely covered with minute, flat, purplish-red scales which are very dense at the centre but pulled apart towards the edge as the cap expands. *Gills* sinuately attached to the stem apex, sulphur yellow, broad, moderately crowded. *Stem* 6–10cm (2–4in), fairly stocky, about 1cm ($\frac{1}{2}$in) thick, cylindrical, solid becoming hollow, with a surface similarly coloured to the cap, with the purple scales becoming less dense towards the top. *Flesh* thick, firm and deep yellow. *Spore-print* white; *spores* ovoid, colourless, smooth.
Edibility: Not poisonous but with an unpleasant bitter taste and therefore cannot be eaten.
General remarks: The bright and contrasting purple and yellow colours make this one of the easier mushrooms to recognise, and it has acquired several popular names such as 'Strawberry Mushroom', 'Plums and Custard' and the 'Variegated Mop'. *Tricholomopsis* species look very like *Tricholoma* but grow on rotting wood. *T. decora* grows in mountainous regions, and has brown, rather than purple scales.

Tricholomopsis rutilans

SHAGGY INK CAP

Coprinus comatus

Description: *Cap* 6–15cm ($2\frac{1}{2}$–6in) tall, cylindric but becoming more bell-shaped as the fungus matures, white with a pale brown apex, covered with tiers of shaggy, fibrous scales with tips turned back. The entire cap gradually dissolves from the margin into a black inky liquid and becomes progressively smaller. *Gills* free, densely crowded, white at the top of stem but becoming pinkish at edge and finally black as the spores mature. *Stem* up to 30cm (12in) high, about 1cm ($\frac{3}{8}$in) thick, cylindric, white, with a ring towards base. *Flesh* thin, white, soft. *Spore-print* black; *spores* ellipsoid with a germ-pore, black, smooth.

Edibility: Excellent when young and gills still white, but older specimens should be discarded. It has been used as a substitute for asparagus. One of the mushrooms eaten in Ancient Rome.

General remarks: Probably the best known of the Ink Caps, called the Shaggy Mane in North America, and the Lawyer's Wig in Britain. They are a unique group of mushrooms, dispersing their spores through liquefaction of the gills. The Common Ink Cap (*C. atramentarius*) is grey and not scaly, with a rounded bell-shaped cap, and is poisonous if eaten with alcohol.

Classification: Basidiomycotina, family Coprinaceae.
Habitat: Occurring in small tufts, often in large numbers, in fields, gardens, roadside verges, and capable of lifting asphalt and paving stones.
Distribution: Common everywhere, probably world-wide.
Season: April–November.

Pholiota squarrosa

Classification: Basidiomycotina, family Strophariaceae.
Habitat: Forming dense clusters at base of deciduous trees.
Distribution: Widespread throughout Europe and North America.
Season: July–December.

Description: *Cap* 3–10cm (1¼–4in) diameter, convex, pale ochre, dry, covered with dense zones of crowded, reddish brown, erect, fibrous, pointed scales. *Gills* adnate, with a decurrent tooth, yellowish then rusty brown, crowded. *Stem* 6–15cm (2½–6in), up to 1.5cm (⅝in) thick, cylindric, covered with similar scales to the cap, and provided with a ring towards the apex. *Flesh* pale cream, firm. *Spore-print* rusty brown; *spores* ovoid with a germ-pore, yellowish brown, smooth.
Edibility: Although young specimens are said to be edible, it is not recommended owing to the bitter taste, and can cause gastric upsets.
General remarks: This is a parasite, entering through wounds in the bark. *Pholiota* species are recognized by the brown gills and spores, the ring on the stem, and usually grow on wood. The Shaggy Pholiota, also known as the Scaly Pholiota or Prickly Cap, is one of the larger species, and is related to the Golden Pholiota (*P. aurivella*), which grows on the upper branches and has a slimy cap, and the Pineapple Pholiota (*P. adiposa*) which only grows on beech and in which both cap and stem are slimy. The Orange Pholiota (*Gymnopilus junonius*) grows in a similar situation to the Shaggy Pholiota but is not scaly.

SICKENER

Russula emetica

Description: *Cap* 4–9cm (1½–3½in) diameter, convex then depressed in the centre, shiny scarlet red, with a smooth, sticky surface, and a coarsely striped edge. *Gills* adnexed, white, moderately crowded. *Stem* 5–8cm (2–3¼in), up to 2cm (¾in) thick, cylindric, fragile, pure white. *Flesh* white, brittle, with a very peppery taste. *Spore-print* pure white; *spores* ovoid, colourless, with warts and ridges which stain blue in iodine.

Edibility: This is also known as the Emetic Russula, and is likely to cause vomiting, especially if eaten raw.

General remarks: Many *Russula* species are brightly coloured, and there are several red species which are easily confused. The Sickener has a relatively long stem, and thin flesh, and need not be mistaken for *R. mairei*, which is similarly coloured, but smaller, thicker fleshed, and always grows with beech trees. *R. paludosa* is the largest of the group, also found in boggy situations, especially amongst peat, but differs in having cream-coloured gills, and a pink-flushed stem. *R. lepida* is a paler red, with cream gills, and grows in beech and oak woods.

Classification: Basidiomycotina, family Russulaceae.

Habitat: On the ground in coniferous woods, especially pine, usually in damp, mossy situations.

Distribution: Widespread, wherever there are coniferous forests or plantations.

Season: July–October.

Calocybe gambosa

Classification: Basidiomycotina, family Tricholomataceae.

Habitat: In meadows and pastures, sometimes around hedges, especially on chalk, and may form large 'fairy-rings'.

Distribution: Widespread in the Northern Hemisphere, but probably more common in Europe.

Season: April–June.

Description: *Cap* 5–12cm (2–4¾in) diameter, slightly convex then expanding and becoming flattened, with an undulating, inrolled edge, whitish or very pale pinkish-brown at centre, smooth, dry. *Gills* sinuate to the stem, white, narrow, densely crowded. *Stem* 4–8cm (1½–3¼in), about 2cm (¾in) thick, short, white, powdery on the upper part. *Flesh* very thick, white, with a strong smell of damp flour. *Spore-print* white; *spores* small, ellipsoid, colourless, smooth.

Edibility: It is said to taste of newly ground meal and is best sampled in soups. Although collected enthusiastically for the table, this is probably due to the time of year rather than to its taste.

General remarks: One of the first mushrooms to appear at about the same time as the Morels (p. 46). It gets its name from its appearance around St. George's Day (23 April), although in France it is called the Spring Mushroom. Care should be taken to avoid picking either *Entoloma sinuatum*, which has a yellowish grey cap and pink gills, or *Inocybe patouillardii*, which has a conical cap and brown gills. Both occur in similar situations to St. George's Mushroom but are poisonous.

UGLY MILK CAP

Lactarius turpis

Description: *Cap* 6–20cm (2½–8in) diameter, convex but soon becoming distinctly depressed in centre, dull olive-brown and almost blackish towards centre, but much paler at edge, with a smooth and slimy surface. *Gills* decurrent on the stem, off-white to straw yellow, quickly becoming discoloured brownish when bruised, crowded. *Stem* short, 4–6cm (1½–2¼in), about 2–3cm (¾–1¼in) thick, paler than cap, sticky. *Flesh* thick, pale brownish, with a very hot peppery taste, and releasing copious white milky liquid when broken. *Spore-print* pale pinkish-buff; *spores* ovoid, colourless, with a netted surface staining blue in iodine.

Edibility: The very hot, peppery taste makes this species unpalatable and indigestible.

General remarks: Although this is very common, it is often overlooked owing to its dull colour. *Lactarius* species, or Milk Caps, represent a large and familiar group of mushrooms in Autumn and can often be difficult to distinguish from each other. The are closely allied to *Russula* species but have decurrent gills and release a milky liquid when flesh or gills are broken.

Classification: Basidiomycotina, family Russulaceae.

Habitat: Always growing with birch, on heathland, often hidden in long grass.

Distribution: Very common in Europe, but much less so or only locally common in North America.

Season: July–October.

Flammulina velutipes

Classification: Basidiomycotina, family Tricholomataceae.

Habitat: Forming small tufts on trunks and branches of deciduous trees, especially elm.

Distribution: Widespread throughout Europe and North America.

Season: September–March.

Description: *Cap* 2–5cm ($\frac{3}{4}$–2in) diameter, convex becoming flat, bright yellowish brown, moist and sticky when wet, becoming shiny when dry, smooth. *Gills* adnexed, pale cream-yellow, well spaced. *Stem* 2–5cm ($\frac{3}{4}$–2in), about 5mm ($\frac{1}{4}$in) thick, cylindrical, pale yellowish at apex but dark brownish below, with a velvety surface. *Flesh* thin, gelatinous, whitish. *Spore-print* white; *spores* ellipsoid, colourless, smooth.

Edibility: The caps are edible after the slimy skin has been removed. It has a strong taste and is usually used in soups. In Japan, it is grown and sold commercially under the name *Eno-take*.

General remarks: This mushroom is remarkable for its ability to survive frost and will continue to grow even after it has been completely frozen. It is known from as far north as Alaska, and is often the only mushroom to be found in Winter and therefore is gathered for food in many countries. It is also important economically as a wound parasite of trees, growing beneath the bark and causing a sapwood rot. The dark velvety stem is the distinguishing character for this species.

WOOD BLEWIT

Lepista nuda

Description: *Cap* 6–12cm (2½–4¾in) diameter, slightly convex but soon becoming flattened, colour variable from uniformly violet like the stem, greyish lilac to reddish brown with violet tints at edge, often appearing water-soaked, smooth. *Gills* sinuately attached to the stem, violet paling to pinkish, moderately crowded. *Stem* 6–8cm (2½–3in) high, about 2cm (¾in) thick, cylindric, bright bluish lilac, fibrous. *Flesh* thick, whitish with a lilac tint, firm. *Spore-print* pale pink; *spores* ellipsoid, colourless, with tiny warts.

Edibility: Good and recommended, with a strong flavour. It is sold commercially in many countries. However, it can be slightly poisonous if eaten raw, and some people are allergic to it.

General remarks: The lilac-violet tints and the pale spore-print easily distinguish the blewits. The Blewit (*L. saeva*) is rarer, usually associated with chalk, and has greyish or whitish gills. *L. sordida* is thinner and paler, with uniformly greyish-lilac cap, gills and stem, and is usually found on compost heaps or disturbed soil.

Classification: Basidiomycotina, family Tricholomataceae.

Habitat: In troops on the ground in deciduous woodland.

Distribution: Widespread and one of the best known mushrooms throughout Europe and North America.

Season: September–December (November–March in western North America).

Classification: Basidiomycotina, family Agaricaceae.

Habitat: On the ground in fields, woods, and under hedges especially in urban areas.

Distribution: Throughout Europe and the west coast of North America.

Season: July–October, (November–March in North America).

Description: *Cap* 5–15cm (2–6in) diameter, at first hemispheric with a flattened top, later expanding to broadly bell-shaped, white, cracking when dry, discolouring bright chrome yellow when bruised. *Gills* free, pale grey becoming dark purplish brown at maturity, broad, crowded. *Stem* 6–15cm (2½–6in), up to 1.5cm (¾in) thick, cylindric with swollen base, white, staining bright yellow, bearing a large, thin ring towards the apex. *Flesh* thick, firm, white but immediately changing to bright yellow at the base of the stem, and with a distinct smell of ink or carbolic. *Spore-print* purplish brown; *spores* ovoid, dark brown, smooth.

Edibility: To be avoided, causing vomiting and other gastric upsets within two hours of ingestion.

General remarks: This is one of the very few true mushrooms which are not edible. However, it is easy to recognize as the bright chrome yellow discoloration of the exposed flesh of the stem base is characteristic, so always remember to include the stem base when collecting. The large ring on the stem is also a good warning. *A. placomyces* is closely related but has small, sooty brown scales on the cap and is found in deciduous woodland.

Agaricus xanthodermus

BITTER BOLETUS

Tylopilus felleus

Description: *Cap* 4–20cm (1½–8in) diameter, convex or uneven to almost flat with a thick margin, pale greyish yellow to dark brown, dull, velvety and eventually cracking when dry. *Tubes* adnately attached to the stem; *pores* round, cream colour to flesh pink, bruising rusty brown. *Stem* 3–15cm (1¼–6in), up to 4cm (1½in) thick, cream to yellowish at the apex, becoming rusty brown below, with ridged brownish net-like veins. *Flesh* thick, white and unchanging or slightly reddish when broken, with an intensely bitter taste. *Spore-print* clay pink; *spores* spindle-shaped, pink, smooth.

Edibility: Not poisonous but the extremely bitter taste makes this mushroom inedible, and it will ruin any dish if included accidentally.

General remarks: It is one of the few boletes to be found under both conifers and deciduous trees. Although the genus *Tylopilus* is well represented in the Southern Hemisphere, this is the only species found in Europe. It is easily confused with the Penny Bun Boletus (p. 36), but that species has a white network pattern on the stem. It is quite safe to taste a small piece of the flesh if you are in doubt.

Classification: Basidiomycotina, family Boletaceae.

Habitat: On the ground, usually on sandy soil, in either coniferous or oak and beech woods, always growing in association with the trees.

Distribution: Widespread but localized throughout Europe and eastern North America.

Season: June–November.

Strobilomyces floccopus

Classification: Basidiomycotina, family Strobilomycetaceae.

Habitat: On the ground in deciduous woodland, especially beech.

Distribution: Throughout Europe and the eastern side of North America but not always common.

Season: August–October.

Description: *Cap* 4–12cm ($1\frac{1}{2}$–$4\frac{3}{4}$in) diameter, hemispherical to convex, densely covered with thick, overlapping blackish, woolly, pyramid-shaped scales on a white background, with a shaggy edge. *Tubes* adnate, pale; *pores* large, pale grey bruising reddish. *Stem* 8–12cm (3–$4\frac{3}{4}$in) high, tall and cylindrical, dark greyish, scaly, with a ring-zone towards the apex. *Flesh* soft, white becoming reddish and finally black. *Spore-print* blackish brown; *spores* almost spherical, very dark brown, with a net-work ornamentation.

Edibility: Young specimens which are entirely white can be eaten but older ones are too tough. Much prized in eastern Europe.

General remarks: The name *Strobilomyces* means the 'pine-cone fungus' and this refers to the overall appearance of the cap with the thick, overlapping scales. It is the only species to be found in Europe but in North America there is the closely related *Strobilomyces confusus* which has erect scales on the cap, and spiny spores. Species of *Strobilomyces* are more common in warmer climates, and the Old Man of the Woods is more frequent in southern Europe.

PENNY BUN BOLETUS

Boletus edulis

Description: *Cap* 10–30cm (4–12in) diameter, strongly convex with a thick margin, chestnut brown but can be much paler or darker, dry but slightly sticky when moist. *Tubes* free or adnexed to the stem; *pores* very small, white becoming greenish yellow. *Stem* 10–20cm (4–10in), up to 4cm (1½in) thick, almost cylindric or very swollen below (up to 10cm (4in) thick), hard, pale brown, covered above with a white net-like pattern. *Flesh* white, unchanging, firm. *Spore-print* clay brown; *spores* spindle-shaped, pale brown, smooth.

Edibility: Excellent, known in France and Italy as 'king of the mushrooms', with a delicious nutty flavour. Much used commercially in soup packets. Do not confuse with the Bitter Boletus (p. 34).

General remarks: Also known as the *Cep* in France, and the *Steinpilz* (Stone Fungus) in Germany. In a good season, it can grow profusely, very quickly, and is also very popular with squirrels. True *Boletus* species are easy to recognise, usually with a pale net-like pattern on the swollen stem. *B. aestivalis* occurs earlier from May onwards and has a cracked, light brown cap, whilst *B. pinicola* grows in coniferous woods and has a dark copper brown cap. The only poisonous species is the Devil's Boletus (*B. satanas*) which has a bright red stem.

Classification: Basidiomycotina, family Boletaceae.

Habitat: On the ground in both beech and oak woods, and also coniferous woods.

Distribution: Widespread and common throughout Europe and North America.

Season: June–November.

Xerocomus chrysenteron

Classification: Basidiomycotina, family Xerocomaceae.
Habitat: Very common, on the ground in deciduous woodland, especially beech and oak woods and by roadsides.
Distribution: Common everywhere throughout the north temperate region.
Season: June–November.

Description: *Cap* 4–8cm (1½–3in) diameter, convex soon becoming flattened or depressed at the centre, reddish brown with an olive-green tint, dry and finely velvety, soon cracking to reveal a pinkish flesh between the cracks. *Tubes* adnate to adnexed; *pores* large and angular, yellow. *Stem* 4–8cm (1½–3in), about 1cm thick, (⅜in), cylindric, yellowish with carmine red longitudinal streaks. *Flesh* soft, creamy yellow but often reddish in the stem, and turning slowly bluish green when cut. *Spore-print* clay brown; *spores* spindle-shaped, pale brown, smooth.
Edibility: Can be eaten but only of moderate quality. The tubes and stem should be removed before cooking.
General remarks: This is one of the most common species, often found in urban areas. It is closely related to the Yellow-cracked Boletus (*X. subtomentosus*), which lacks the carmine red colour. There are a number of *Xerocomus* species, all very similar with a velvety cap, and a slender stem. *X. armeniacus* has a peach-coloured cap, whilst in *X. pruinatus* it is almost blackish. The Bay Boletus (*X. badius*), which occurs in coniferous woods, has a chestnut brown cap, and the flesh discolours blue when broken.

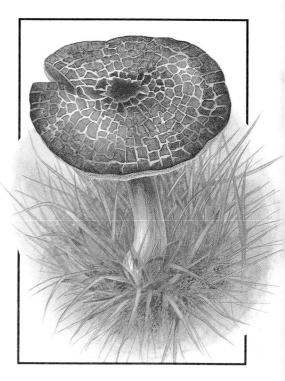

SLIPPERY JACK

Suillus luteus

Description: *Cap* 7–12cm (2¾–4¾in) diameter, convex or slightly raised at the centre, dark chocolate brown to purplish brown, paler when old, very slimy when moist. *Tubes* adnate to decurrent, short and yellow; *pores* sulphur yellow, becoming angular. *Stem* 6–10cm (2½–4in), up to 2cm (¾in) thick, cylindric or tapering at base, solid, yellow but covered with dark brown granules, and with a large white, slimy ring at the apex which eventually collapses to leave a zone. *Flesh* pale yellow in the cap, darker in the stem, soft. *Spore-print* olive brown; *spores* short spindle-shaped, pale brown, smooth.

Edibility: It has a mild taste and can be eaten but regarded by most people as indigestible. It is also prone to insect attack. The slimy skin must be removed before cooking.

General comments: The Ancient Romans called all boletes *fungi suilli* (Pig Fungi), and this is the origin of the name *Suillus*. The boletes are always associated with conifers and have slimy caps. Slippery Jack is very closely related to the Larch Boletus (*S. grevillei*) which is found growing in grass, always under larch, and differs in the paler cap, larger pores and no granules on the stem.

Classification: Basidiomycotina, family Boletaceae.

Habitat: On sandy soil, in coniferous woodland, especially associated with Scots Pine, and probably also with firs.

Distribution: Common throughout Europe and eastern North America.

Season: July–October.

Cantharellus cibarius

Classification: Basidiomycotina, family Cantharellaceae.
Habitat: Often in large numbers, on sand or clay soils in beech and oak woods, sometimes with birch, pine or firs.
Distribution: Widespread throughout Europe and North America.
Season: July–November.

Description: *Cap* 3–10cm (1¼–4in) diameter, flattened soon developing a depressed centre to become funnel-shaped, bright egg-yellow, smooth, moist, with a wavy, inrolled margin. *Gills* decurrent on the stem, shallow, fold-like, branching and interconnected, egg-yellow to orange, with a blunt edge, widely spaced. *Stem* 2–5cm (¾–2in), 0.5–1.5cm (¼–¾in) thick, short, tapering below, often compressed, smooth, egg-yellow. *Flesh* thin, soft but firm, with a pleasant dried apricot smell. *Spore-print* very pale pinkish; *spores* ovoid, colourless, smooth.
Edibility: Excellent, and much prized. Widely sold in markets and much used in restaurants. Can be preserved by drying, but is best cooked in the fresh state, slowly in butter.
General remarks: Not always found and seems to require plenty of rain. A very easy species to recognize owing to the uniform egg-yellow colour. It is only likely to be confused with the False Chanterelle (*Hygrophoropsis aurantiaca*), which is more common, found in coniferous woods, and has true gills instead of thick ridges. Another species of conifer woods is the Autumn Chanterelle (*Cantharellus tubaeformis*), which can occur in enormous numbers and is collected commercially in Finland.

HORN OF PLENTY

Craterellus cornucopioides

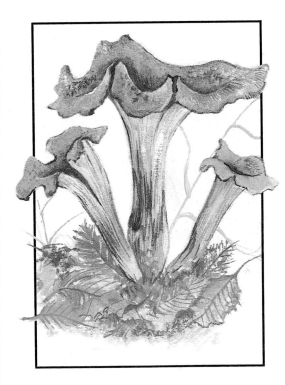

Description: *Cap* 2–8cm (¾–3in) diameter, tubular and trumpet-shaped, lobed, with the edge flared, sooty-brown to black, felty with small scales, *Gills* none, but a smooth or slightly wrinkled outer surface, slate grey or bluish grey with a waxy aspect. *Stem* 2–4cm (¾–1½in) high, indistinctly separated from the cap, compressed, blackish brown. *Flesh* very thin, brittle, grey, with a pleasant fruity smell. *Spore-print* white; *spores* ellipsoid, colourless, smooth.

Edibility: Good, and described in France as the 'meat of the poor'. Usually cut up for cooking, and often used in a dried, powdered form.

General remarks: The dark colours make this species difficult to find in the woods, and when it is wet it becomes virtually black, resembling old, dirty leather. The dull colour has given it the name Trumpet of Death. It does grow in large numbers, however, and is much sought after for its excellent flavour. In North America, this species is sometimes replaced by the Black Trumpet (*C. fallax*) which has slightly different coloured spores.

Classification: Basidiomycotina, family Craterellaceae.

Habitat: In troops amongst leaf litter, normally in beech woods but also in coniferous woods.

Distribution: Widespread throughout Europe and eastern North America.

Season: August–October.

Scleroderma citrinum (S. aurantium)

Classification: Basidiomycotina, family Scleromycetaceae.
Habitat: Common on sandy heathland and amongst leaf-mould in woods.
Distribution: Widespread throughout Europe and North America.
Season: August–October.

Description: *Fruitbody* 2.5–10cm (1–4in) diameter, hemispherical but often flattened above, dirty yellowish brown and soon cracking into regular, rough, scale-like areas; attached to the soil by a mass of coarse, root-like cottony threads. When cut open there is seen to be a thick whitish outer fleshy layer (*peridium*), which turns pink, and contains the solid spore mass (*gleba*), which is at first white, appears marbled, then becomes purplish black, gradually becoming powdery and brownish as the spores mature. The outer layer finally splits open at the top and the spores are blown away by the wind. *Spores* round, dark brown, with a net-like ornament.
Edibility: This is poisonous, and can cause nausea and vomiting when consumed in large quantities. In North America it is known as the Pigskin Poison Puffball.
General remarks: This is the most common species of *Scleroderma*. It grows either as individual fruitbodies or as small tufts. Sometimes the fruitbodies are parasitized by the Parasitic Bolete (*Xerocomus parasiticus*), an unusual example of one fungus species growing as a parasite on another. *Xerocomus verrucosum* has a distinct stalk-like base and much smaller scales over the surface.

GIANT PUFF-BALL

Langermannia gigantea

Description: *Fruitbody* up to 50cm (20in) or more in diameter, generally about the size of a football, with a smooth and white surface. The interior is at first white and firm but as the spores mature the colour changes to yellowish to olive-brown and the texture becomes cottony and powdery. The fruitbody is at first attached to the soil by a fine cord, but often this is broken away. The surface progressively flakes away over several weeks and the mature spores are blown away by the wind. *Spores* round, yellowish brown, with minute warts.

Edibility: One of the most tasty species when the fruitbody is young and the contents are white and firm. Generally prepared by cutting into slices, about 1cm ($\frac{1}{2}$in) thick, and gently frying in butter.

General remarks: This is the largest of all the puff-balls and is remarkable in the millions of spores produced by just one fruitbody. An estimate for an average specimen is 7,000 million, and an overall weight of 18kg (40lb) is not uncommon. The dried cottony contents of old puff-balls have historically been used as a styptic.

Classification: Basidiomycotina, family Lycoperdaceae.

Habitat: Solitary or occasionally in large numbers in grassland, woods, often on disturbed soil or by roadsides.

Distribution: Locally common throughout Europe and eastern North America. Fruitbodies can reappear in the same place each year, sometimes forming 'fairy-rings'.

Season: August–October.

Phallus impudicus

Classification: Basidiomycotina, family Phallaceae.
Habitat: On the ground, attached by underground white, mycelial cords to wood fragments or old roots, in woodlands, especially beech woods.
Distribution: Common in Europe and western North America.
Season: July–October.

Description: *Fruitbody* is a sticky cap born on a tall stem. *Cap* 2–4cm ($\frac{3}{4}$–1$\frac{1}{2}$in) high, conical with a branched system of coarse ridges, white but covered by a dark olive-brown slime (gleba), which has an extremely pungent smell of rotting meat. *Stem* 10–14cm (4–5$\frac{1}{2}$in) high, about 2–3cm ($\frac{3}{4}$–1$\frac{1}{4}$in) thick, cylindric, hollow, spongy, white to pale cream colour. *Volva* appearing like a white, soft egg ('witch's egg') when immature, then rupturing above to release the fruitbody which grows very quickly. *Spores* rod-shaped, colourless, smooth.
Edibility: Generally not regarded as edible but in eastern Europe the young, unopened egg is sometimes sliced and used in salads. The mature fruitbodies are regarded as a delicacy in China.
General remarks: The first indication of this fungus is a pungent smell noticed on entering a wood. The smell is produced to attract insects, especially flies, which disperse the sticky spores. There is much folk-lore attached to the fruitbodies, especially the eggs, and they have been used in Europe as a treatment for gout, arthritis and rheumatism, and, of course, as an aphrodisiac.

CRESTED CLAVARIA

Clavulina cristata

Description: *Fruitbody* 2–7cm ($\frac{3}{4}$–$2\frac{3}{4}$in) high, erect with a short, stout, stem-like base, highly branched, flattened, with tooth-like, jagged, pointed, apical branches, white, sometimes tinted yellow or greyish, firm, with a pleasant smell. *Spore-print* white; *spores* ovoid, colourless, smooth.

Edibility: Edible and regarded as quite pleasant, but coral-fungi generally are not regarded as edible.

General remarks: This mushroom, which grows singly or in groups, is one of the most common species of the coral-fungi, and in North America it is known as the Crested Coral. The genus *Clavulina* contains about six species, all very similar. The Grey Coral (*C. cinerea*) is often confused and differs only in a more greyish colour, whilst *C. rugosa* is more robust, pale grey, with only a few thick, flattened, wrinkled branches. The club-fungi and coral-fungi are a familiar group in both woodlands and grassland. Some species, such as *Clavulinopsis fusiformis*, are bright yellow and unbranched, whilst many of the *Ramaria* species form large, dense coral-like tufts. Some *Ramaria* species are regarded as mildly poisonous. Another striking species in beech woods is *Clavariadelphus pistillaris*, which forms a large, thick, simple club, up to 15cm (6in) high.

Classification: Basidiomycotina, family Clavulinaceae.

Habitat: On the ground in deciduous and coniferous woodland, often found beside paths.

Distribution: Throughout Europe and North America.

Season: June–October.

Auricularia auricula-judae

Classification: Basidiomycotina, family Auriculariaceae.
Habitat: Common, either solitary or in groups on branches of deciduous trees, particularly Elder, but occasionally on other trees.
Distribution: Widespread throughout Europe but less common in North America.
Season: January–December.

Description: *Fruitbody* 3–10cm (1¼–4in) diameter, resembling a human ear, with the upper surface dark date brown to blackish and smooth, jelly-like but firm and rubbery to the touch, finely velvety. *Underside* with irregular folds and ridges, pale purplish brown. *Stem* none, laterally attached. *Flesh* thin, gelatinous. *Spore-print* white; *spores* curved, cylindric, colourless, smooth.
Edibility: The very closely related Kikurage or Mo-Ehr (*Auricularia polytricha*) is much used in Chinese and Japanese cuisine, although more for the chewy texture than for its flavour, and possibly for medicinal and therapeutic properties.
General remarks: The common name relates to the Judas Tree, or Elder, and the mushroom was originally called Judas's Ear. A pure white form is occasionally found. *Auricularia mesenterica* forms overlapping brackets, with a hairy, zoned, upper surface. The jelly fungi are so-called because of their soft texture and a high water content in wet weather, but they can dry out and become difficult to see when dry. Most grow on dead wood and stumps. *Tremella* species are convoluted and brain-like, and either yellow or brown, whilst the yellow *Calocera* species look like small club-fungi. *Dacrymyces* form small, yellow spots.

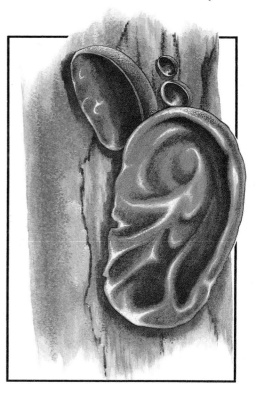

COMMON MOREL

Morchella esculenta

Description: *Cap* 3–7cm (1¼–2¾in) high, about 2–4cm (¾–1½in) broad, conical or more rounded, yellowish brown to greyish brown, hollow, with a coarse, regular network of thick ridges, and an indefinite edge which joins the stem. *Stem* 2–17cm (¾–6¾in) high, about 2cm (¾in) thick, cylindric, at times with a swollen base, whitish to yellow, with indefinite ribs, surface rough and granular. *Flesh* thin, fibrous, with a mild, pleasant smell. *Spore-print* deep cream; *spores* ellipsoid, colourless, smooth.

Edibility: Greatly prized, especially in dried form, and one of the few mushrooms available in Spring. Sold extensively in France and Germany. The greatest care, however, must be taken in avoiding the Turban Fungus (*Gyromitra esculenta*) which has a brown, rounded, brain-like cap instead of the regular ridges found in the Morel.

General remarks: Morels tend to be much more common in North America, where they can be collected by the bushel, and sometimes giant specimens are encountered. There are many forms and varieties of the Common Morel, and they are difficult to distinguish. *M. elata* is tall and thin, whilst *M. conica* has a very cone-like cap.

Classification: Ascomycotina, family Morchellaceae.
Habitat: On rich, often cultivated or disturbed soil, also likes burnt ground.
Distribution: Throughout Europe and North America, but less common in more northerly localities.
Season: April–June.